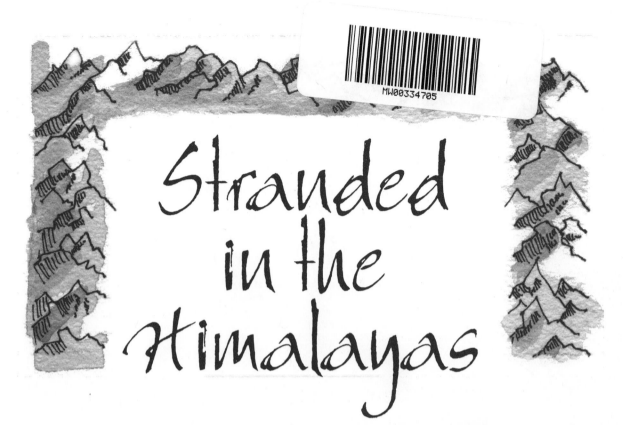

Stranded in the Himalayas

Leader's Manual

Lorraine L. Ukens

Jossey-Bass
Pfeiffer

MW00334705

Copyright © 1998 by Jossey-Bass/Pfeiffer

ISBN: 0-7879-3969-2

Library of Congress Catalog Card Number 97-75841

All rights reserved. No part of this publication may be reproduced, stored in a retrieval system, or transmitted, in any form or by any means, electronic, mechanical, photocopying, recording, or otherwise, without the prior written permission of the publisher.

Printed in the United States of America

Published by

350 Sansome Street, 5th Floor
San Francisco, California 94104-1342
(415) 433-1740; Fax (415) 433-0499
(800) 274-4434; Fax (800) 569-0443

Visit our website at: http://www.pfeiffer.com

Outside of the United States, Pfeiffer products can be purchased from the following Simon & Schuster International Offices:

Simon & Schuster (Asia) Pte Ltd
317 Alexandra Road
#04-01 IKEA Building
Singapore 159965
Asia
65 476 4688; Fax 65 378 0370

Prentice Hall
Campus 400
Maylands Avenue
Hemel Hempstead
Hertfordshire HP2 7EZ
United Kingdom
44(0) 1442 881891; Fax 44(0) 1442 882288

Prentice Hall Professional
Locked Bag 507
Frenchs Forest PO NSW 2086
Australia
61 2 9454 2200; Fax 61 2 9453 0089

Prentice Hall/Pfeiffer
P.O. Box 1636
Randburg 2125
South Africa
27 11 781 0780; Fax 27 11 781 0781

Acquiring Editor: Matt Holt
Director of Development: Kathleen Dolan Davies
Developmental Editor: Susan Rachmeler
Copyeditor: Rebecca Taff
Senior Production Editor: Dawn Kilgore
Interior Design: Joseph Piliero
Cover Design: Paula Goldstein
Illustrations: Mark Deneen

Printing   10   9   8   7   6   5   4   3   2

 This book is printed on acid-free, recycled stock that meets or exceeds the minimum GPO and EPA requirements for recycled paper.

Contents

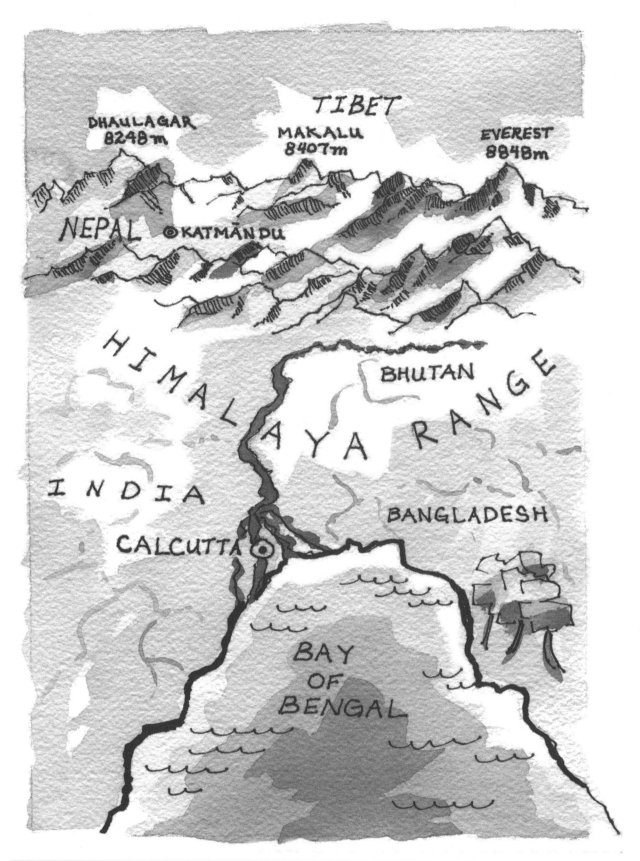

Jossey-Bass/Pfeiffer

When to Use
Stranded in the Himalayas

The subject of this simulation (survival in the Himalayan mountains) is not the topic for learning. It merely provides an interesting, effective, and entertaining way to introduce work teams or other groups to the concepts of consensus and synergy in decision making, although the information about survival and decisions in emergency situations also may be of interest and value to the participants.

This simulation provides immediate feedback to group members on how well they perform as a team. It can be used effectively in training for any of the following purposes:

Consensus Decision Making

This simulation provides a group or intact work team with an opportunity to learn how to make decisions by consensus. This may be a new experience for some participants, because group decisions are frequently made by voting, trading, or negotiating. In many cases, however, a satisfactory decision can be reached only by consensus. If members of a group need to become more familiar with the process of consensus decision making, this simulation will enable them to experience the various aspects of the process and will reinforce its value.

Synergistic Decision Making

This simulation explores the concept of synergy with regard to the results of group decision making versus the results of individual decision making. It also provides first-hand experience of the value in synergistic processes for enhancing the variety of options considered as well as the quality of the final decision. The activity requires participants to use both interpersonal and rational skills in reaching group decisions.

General Problem Solving and Decision Making

In any effort to teach problem-solving and decision-making skills, this simulation provides an interesting and engaging situation for both individuals and groups.

Comparing Individual Decisions with Team Decisions

This simulation will illustrate the benefit of using all the resources of a team rather than relying solely on the ability of one or two members to generate ideas, solve a problem, or make a decision. The process of analyzing both team and individual scores helps participants gain insight into their own problem-solving abilities as well as their impact on group decision making.

Teamwork

Participants will gain experience in interpersonal skills as they work together to arrive at decisions during this activity. It will give them an opportunity to examine the impact of their own behaviors on team effectiveness. Participants will be able to provide one another with both supportive and critical feedback in a nonthreatening environment.

By observing the group process, the facilitator also will have an opportunity to provide the group as a whole with feedback on its approach to the task, its processes, and its interpersonal dynamics.

Group Behavior

This simulation can be used to explore many other aspects of group behavior, such as participation, group member styles, leadership styles, conflict resolution, and communication skills.

Administration of
Stranded in the Himalayas

Goals

- To practice the consensus decision-making process in a task group.

- To explore the concept of synergy with regard to the outcomes of group decision making.

- To examine the various aspects of group behavior that occur in a team situation.

Group Size

Five to eight participants per group. Several groups may be directed simultaneously in the same room.

Time Required

Approximately 1½ hours.

Materials

- One copy of the *Stranded in the Himalayas* activity for each participant.

- A pencil or pen for each participant.

- A clipboard or desk chair for each participant.

- A newsprint flip chart and felt-tipped markers.

- A newsprint sheet showing the "correct" answers.

- Charts for scoring (see pages 6 and 7). The charts should be prepared in advance, with scores recorded after participants complete the simulation.

Physical Setting

A room large enough for the entire group, with enough space that subgroups can work without distracting one another. A table may be provided for each subgroup. (Although tables can be used for individual work, the dynamics involved are likely to be somewhat different.)

Process

1. Distribute one copy of the *Stranded in the Himalayas* activity, a pencil or pen, and a clipboard to each person. Explain to the participants that they should not break the seal at the back of the booklet until instructed to do so and that they should work independently during the first phase (i.e., Your Task). Ask them to read the instructions for The Situation and for Your Task on pages 1 and 2 of their booklets; allow sufficient time for reading. Explain that they will have fifteen minutes in which to complete the task, then give them a signal to begin.

2. After thirteen minutes, give a two-minute warning. After the two minutes, instruct the participants to stop working.

3. Divide the participants into subgroups of five to eight members each, depending on the size of the total group. Identify each subgroup by number, name, or letter of the alphabet. Direct the subgroups to separate tables or areas of the room.

4. Introduce the concept and objective of consensus decision making (based on pages 13 and 14 of this manual). Instruct the participants to read the Guidelines for

---

Reaching Consensus, beginning on page 7 of their booklets. Allow sufficient time for them to finish reading the guidelines.

5. Tell the participants that each subgroup's task is to reach consensus. Instruct them to open their booklets to the Group's Task on page 8, and review the instructions with them. Emphasize that they will have thirty minutes to reach their consensus decisions, then signal for the subgroups to begin the task.

6. After twenty-five minutes, give the participants a five-minute warning, then a two-minute warning. When the time is up, instruct the subgroups to stop working.

7. Explain that the participants will have a chance to discuss the rationale behind the "correct" answers, but for the moment they should be concerned only with recording them and determining their scores. Post the correct answers, but not the rationale.

8. Tell the participants that the individual answers should be scored first. Read aloud the following instructions and guide the participants through the scoring process:

> Turn to page 2 and write the letter (a, b, or c) that corresponds with the correct answer in the space provided under the heading "Correct Answer." Compare these with letters in the "Your Answer" column and circle every letter that is the same. Total the number of circles and write this number in the appropriate space on page 6. This total represents your individual score.

> When everyone in your subgroup has obtained his or her own score, add everyone's scores together and divide the total by the number of members in your subgroup. The quotient should be carried out to one decimal place. This provides the average individual score for your subgroup; write this number in the space provided on page 12. Check with members of your group to verify that everyone has obtained the same average score to one decimal place. Later, you will be asked to give the facilitator the average individual score and the highest individual score for your group.

Allow sufficient time for this portion of the scoring to occur.

9. Tell participants that they will now calculate the group's score. Read the following instructions out loud:

> Now turn to page 2 and repeat the scoring process for the Group's Task. Circle all the correct letters in the column labeled "Your Group's Answer," add the number of circles, and enter the total in the appropriate space. This number represents your group's total score when using the consensus-decision method. Be ready to give the facilitator this score when requested.

Allow sufficient time for scoring the Group's Task section.

10. Remind the participants that the goal was not to test their knowledge of mountain survival; it was to allow them to explore the process of group consensus. Instruct the participants to break the seals at the back of their booklets and to read the rationale for each answer. Give them about ten minutes to discuss the rationale within their subgroups.

11. Post the large copy of the Individual Decisions Tally Sheet (see following) and direct participants to the last page of their booklets. Obtain both the Average Individual Score and the Highest Individual Score from each subgroup, recording the numbers in the appropriate spaces. Determine the averages for all groups combined in both of these categories and enter the numbers on the last line of the chart. [*Note:* The average is obtained by adding all the scores, then dividing by the number of groups participating.]

INDIVIDUAL DECISIONS TALLY SHEET		
Group	**Average Individual Score**	**Highest Individual Score**
Example	7.3	9
Group 1		
Group 2		
Group 3		
Group 4		
Group 5		
Group 6		
Average for all groups		

12. Now post the large copy of the Group Decisions Tally Sheet (see following) and ask each subgroup to report the group's Total Score. Record these in the Score for Group Consensus column. Referring back to the Individual Decisions Tally Sheet, subtract the Group Consensus Score for each subgroup from the Average Individual Score to determine the Gain/Loss Score. If the group score is higher, enter a + sign (positive) and the numerical difference; if it is lower, enter a − sign (negative) and the number. Follow the same procedure for the Highest Individual Score for each subgroup.

GROUP DECISIONS TALLY SHEET				
Group	Score for Group Consensus	Gain/Loss Over Average Individual Score	Gain/Loss Over Highest Individual Score	Synergy
Example	*10*	*+2.7*	*+1*	*Yes*
Group 1				
Group 2				
Group 3				
Group 4				
Group 5				
Group 6				
Average for all groups				

13. Introduce the concept of synergy (refer to pages 15 and 16 of this manual). Ask the participants how the comparison of the individual scores with the subgroups' scores supports or refutes this concept. For each subgroup, note on the Group Decision Tally Sheet whether or not the subgroup score seems to indicate a synergistic outcome (as shown in the example). Using the two charts to compare the average for all groups, discuss the average performance of the group as a whole.

14. Use the following questions to guide the participants through a discussion:

   • What behaviors helped the consensus-seeking process?

   • What behaviors hindered the consensus-seeking process?

   • What patterns of decision making occurred?

   • Were some group members more influential than others? How did this happen?

   • How did the group discover and use its information resources? Were these resources fully utilized?

   • For groups that experienced synergy, what occurred during deliberations that facilitated this outcome?

   • For any groups that did not experience synergy, what happened during deliberations that may have inhibited its occurrence?

   • In what kinds of situations would consensus decision making be most effective?

- What are the implications of consensus seeking and synergistic outcomes for intact task groups such as committees and management groups?

- What effects might this process have on the group's attitudes?

Variations

1. Participants may give copies of their individual decisions to the facilitator for scoring while they proceed with the group task.

2. Sequential consensus exercises may be used, so that subgroups build on what was learned in the first phase. New subgroups can be formed for the second round.

3. Process observers can be assigned to give feedback about group behavior and/or individual behavior. Use the following chart to record observations:

Members' Names

POSITIVE BEHAVIORS									
Suggests procedures, shares leadership									
Shows enthusiasm									
Encourages others to participate									
Provides information and opinions									
Helps the team to assess its performance									
Praises or supports others									
NEGATIVE BEHAVIORS									
Acts withdrawn or unwilling to participate									
Becomes angry or sulks									
Shows off, seeks individual attention									
Disrupts or disturbs the team process									
Asserts control of the group process									
Criticizes or ridicules others									

Answers and Rationale

Following are the recommended answers for each of the predicaments in *Stranded in the Himalayas*. They are based on information provided by experts on mountaineering and wilderness survival. The responses are considered to be the best rules of thumb for most situations. Specific situations, however, might require different courses of action.

1. (a) Small Frozen Waterfall

Since you have an ice axe and crampons, going down the middle of the ice structure is the safest and easiest route to take because it is solid and out of the route of avalanches. Because rocks absorb more warmth, the snow in an area that borders rock may have softened, and you could plunge through the extremely deep snow. During heavy snowfalls, soft snow can build snowdrifts across crevasses. This snow bridge is formed from both above and below to create a hardened surface. However, a snow bridge is misleading because it often is not strong enough to support the weight of a person. Only arches of ice spanning crevasses are completely solid. A fall into a crevasse is usually fatal, either from the initial impact or from exposure to cold.

---

2. (c) Melt Snow Between Your Gloved Hands and Sip the Water

You will need to use body heat to melt the snow. Ice or snow should never be eaten; it should be melted between your covered hands or other body parts, preferably into a container. You should not place the snow directly against bare skin or in the mouth because this will cause rapid heat loss. In addition, direct contact with ice or snow can cause minor cold injury to lips and mouth.

3. (c) Figs

A high carbohydrate, low protein diet is recommended for periods of exertion in high-altitude, cold conditions. Other than chocolate, the best things to eat are dried fruits and vegetables, which contain 80 to 90 percent water and are pure carbohydrates. You must avoid bran, because it has cellulose that cannot be broken down by digestive juices; this may sometimes have a troubling laxative effect. Meats are high in protein, but they supply energy only at the end of a long and complex metabolic process. Dried fruits, such as figs, are easy to digest and provide an excellent boost of carbohydrates and minerals that are necessary in a dynamic survival situation such as this.

4. (b) Cotton Long-Sleeved Undershirt

Dampness increases the effects of cold. Excessive perspiration causes salt deficiency that can induce cramps or fatigue as well as dehydration. In cold environments, perspiration wetness on underclothes causes excessive chilling, which can lead to hypothermia. Body heat loss is speeded by conduction where wet clothing touches the skin. Because cotton wicks, it draws sweat away from the body, but then retains the water. When wet, cotton is cold and slow to dry because of the complete saturation of the fibers. Wool insulates better because it does not absorb moisture and has the unique property of keeping the body warm, even when wet. Your head should never be uncovered for any length of time because it loses more than 30 percent of its heat. A hat will also provide protection from sunburn and heatstroke, which can occur as a result of the reflective mountain rocks and snow.

5. (b) A Thirty-Minute Nap Every Three to Four Hours

The length of time spent sleeping can be reduced to as little as two hours of every twenty-four without impairing vigilance, as long as it is taken in short naps. The best way is to sleep in a series of twenty- to thirty-minute naps. (The minimum length of time needed to be refreshed by sleep is only ten minutes.) Physical exertion eliminates residual sleepiness and reduces the amount of sleep necessary to recuperate. In addition, short periods of sleep will help prevent the adverse chilling effects of not moving in the extreme cold.

6. (a) Hold Your Fingers Under Your Armpits

The best way to treat frostbite is to place the affected area in lukewarm water or hold it under your armpits. Irreparable damage can be caused by rubbing your hands together, rubbing them with snow, using hot water, or holding them near fire. These methods produce excessive heat and abrasion, which can cause serious tissue damage.

7. (c) Sit on a Small Pile of Stones away from the Rock Wall

Lightning strikes are frequent in the mountains. Any tall or sharp-edged object, holes, fissures, caves, or shelters from overhangs are likely targets for lightning and should be avoided. Because the mountain itself can conduct electricity, sitting away from the rock wall keeps the body's points of contact farther away in case the mountain is struck by lightning. The small pile of stones provides insulation from ground currents.

8. (a) Begin To Do the Backstroke into the Oncoming Snow

When the avalanche reaches you, it will knock you over as it heads down the mountain at sixty miles an hour or more, completely burying you in snow and ice. As long as it is moving, however, you will be able to move too. The best way to do that in snow is to "swim" on your back. Keeping your head up as much as possible to stay near the surface, use your arms and legs to kick and pull yourself upward as the snow goes around you.

9. (b) Start To Dig Your Way Out

Do not wait until the avalanche stops to try to save your life. Continue to move your legs as much as possible and for as long as possible while the avalanche is moving. Avalanches are made of light, powdery snow; once they stop, the snow can freeze so hard it will be like concrete. While the avalanche is moving slowly, start to dig. It is very important to make an air space so that you can breathe. If you have trouble digging, put your hands over your mouth and nose to keep the snow away from your face and leave some air to breathe.

10. (b) Spit To Determine Which Way Your Saliva Falls

You will not be able to tell if you are upside down. Since the snow will be packed tightly, no warm air will be able to get through. If you cannot see any light coming from the surface, then spit. Gravity will cause the saliva to fall toward the ground. After you know which way is down, dig in the opposite direction until you reach the surface.

11. (c) Eat a Candy Bar

Although body heat is produced by moving muscles, do not force yourself to continue moving when you are overly tired. Physical exhaustion and increased hypoglycemia (low blood-sugar level) are prime factors in accelerating the onset of hypothermia. Cold and high-altitude environments cause additional stress that makes demands on carbohydrates in the same way as physical exertion. Since the body uses its sugar reserves before any of the others, the energy supplied by the candy bar (sucrose) would help the body to quickly replace these. Mild exercise will help you warm up, but you must not continue to walk if you are exhausted. Fatigue and sweating will aggravate the situation. Alcohol should be avoided for several reasons: it supplies "empty" calories (devoid of vitamins and minerals); it acts as a toxin that severely diminishes tolerance to cold; it induces drowsiness; and it causes an increase in the diameter of the blood vessels to warm the extremities at the expense of central organs, wherein hypothermia will be encouraged.

12. (c) The Lowest Point of the Slope

The path of an avalanche has three segments: a "release zone" at the top, where the avalanche begins and the snow accelerates; a middle section or "track," where the snow maintains a steady velocity; and a "run-out zone" at the bottom, where the snow decelerates. The top two zones are the most hazardous because avalanches gather speed at the top due to gravity. The safest place to be is at the bottom, where the snow is denser and more stable.

Reading Resources

Donnelly, J., & Kramer, S. (1995). *Survive! Could you?*. New York: Random House.

Maniguet, X. (1994). *Survival: How to prevail in hostile environments* (Ivanka Roberts, Trans.). New York: Facts on File, Inc. (Original work published 1988)

McManners, H. (1994) *The complete wilderness training book*. New York: Dorling Kindersley Publishing, Inc.

Sierra Club (San Diego Chapter). (1993). *Wilderness basics: The complete handbook for hikers and backpackers* (2nd ed.). Seattle: The Mountaineers.

Guidelines for Reaching Consensus

Consensus is a method of reaching agreement in problem-solving and decision-making groups by which everyone discusses the issues and reaches a decision all can support. It incorporates the knowledge and experience, ideas and feelings of all members of a group. Because any final decision must be supported to some degree by each member of the group, all members work together on a mutually acceptable solution, rather than producing a "we-they" division.

Through open discussion, the group identifies alternative courses of action and seeks out new information that it can use to evaluate these alternatives. If it is working effectively, the group will consider both the positive and negative consequences of the alternatives it identifies and will consider options that it initially dismissed as unacceptable. Group decision making is usually superior to individual decision making for tasks that require judgments when there is no "expert" present. When solving a problem requires generating a variety of ideas and evaluating ambiguous situations, groups usually will outperform individuals.

Decision by consensus may be difficult to attain and may take more time than other methods. The group becomes focused on the problem at hand, rather than depending on individual points of view. This approach to problem solving and decision making often results in a higher-quality decision than do other methods, such as majority rule (voting), minority power (persuasion), or compromise. Although there often are easier methods of decision making, they may not include such a careful weighing of all the relevant information.

Because people who are involved in making a decision generally become more committed to it, use of group consensus usually increases acceptance of the decision by the group. It is even possible for a low-quality solution with strong group commitment to be more effective than a high-quality solution without group commitment.

In the consensus-seeking process, you are asked to do the following:

1. *Think through your own ideas* as well as you can before meeting with the group (but realize that others may know information that you do not).

2. *Express your own opinions and explain yourself fully,* so that the rest of the group has the benefit of all members' thinking.

3. *Listen to the opinions and feelings of all other group members* and be ready to modify your own position on the basis of logic and understanding.

4. *Avoid arguing for your own position* in order to "win" as an individual; what is "right" is the best collective judgment of the group as a whole.

5. *View disagreements or conflict as helping to clarify the issue,* rather than as hindering the process. Do not "give in" if you still have serious reservations about an issue; instead, work toward resolution.

6. *Recognize that tension-reducing behaviors, such as laughing or kidding, can be useful,* as long as meaningful conflict is not smoothed over prematurely.

7. *Refrain from conflict-reducing techniques* such as voting, averaging, trading, compromising, or giving in to keep the peace.

8. *Monitor interactions among people* as the group attempts to complete its work and initiate discussions of what really is going on.

9. *Do not assume that an answer is correct* just because there is agreement initially. Discuss the reasons for the answer and explore all possibilities.

The best results come from a fusion of information, logic, and emotion. Consensus seeking is a way to use group resources to produce synergistic outcomes without denying the integrity of individual members.

Synergy

Groups have some obvious advantages over individuals when it comes to making decisions. One is that a number of individuals with differing perspectives can contribute ideas and suggestions. The contribution of one member may catalyze or alter others' thinking, indirectly aiding their own contributions to the group's decision. Additionally, group members can stimulate and encourage one another. This mutual influence process is called *synergy:* the combined action of two or more agents that, acting jointly, increase the effectiveness of one another and produce an outcome that is greater than the sum of their outcomes when acting independently. Therefore, this group process often results in gains in energy and effectiveness that go beyond what would be expected from the combined efforts of separate individuals.

Synergy can be expected when the members of a group work together on a consensus-seeking task. Their combined knowledge, judgment, and problem-solving and decision-making abilities generally produce a score that is better (i.e., more "correct") than the average individual score. However, the fact that several people meet together and produce a solution does not necessarily mean that all their abilities have been utilized. Synergy is more likely to occur when the group follows the Guidelines for Reaching Consensus.

The concept of group synergy means looking at outcomes in a noncompetitive way. It requires breaking out of a dysfunctional either/or mentality and creating a functional type of competition (i.e., stimulation). Winning becomes a group effort rather than an individual quest. Conflict is viewed as an asset rather than as something to be avoided. The members look for bridges between ideas, for wholes rather than parts. Collaboration in generating ideas, planning, and problem solving creates consensual validation of individuals' points of view and sparks more ideas.

Groups achieve synergy when the process of working heightens sharing and contributing. When members truly listen to one another, share ideas and opinions, stay on the topic, and attend to group process, they are more likely to achieve synergy. In a consensus task, the possibility of synergy is increased because the group works together to reach substantial agreement.

However, it is unlikely that a group will produce a synergistic outcome if members carry on more than one conversation at a time, interrupt one another, jump from one subject to another, and/or allow some members not to participate. Strong personality types and high-status group members may dominate the discussion, causing less assertive and lower-status members to go along with them. Groups may then develop *groupthink* —concurrence-seeking behavior. Groupthink may occur when members of decision-making groups try to avoid being too critical in their judgment of others' ideas and focus too heavily on concurring. To enjoy synergy, the group members must not only work toward producing the best solution, but they must also pay close attention to the process that they are using to reach that solution.

What energy is to the individual, synergy is to the group. The synergy of a group always is potentially greater than the sum of the combined energies of its members. The group effort often produces better results than the group's most competent member could have achieved alone. Effective work teams not only use their energy effectively, but they create new energy.

More Great Resources from Jossey-Bass/Pfeiffer!

Strengthen team bonds with friendly competition

Working Together
55 Team Games

Lorraine L. Ukens

Take your team to a higher level of performance with a healthy dose of competition. These stimulating activities provide lessons in determination, teamwork, and planning—all critical elements in achieving high performance.

These simple games will help you:

- **Encourage** members to cooperate and use all members' abilities
- **Motivate** individuals to maximize their contribution
- **Demonstrate** the benefits of cooperative competition
- **Prepare** your team to meet future challenges
- **Emphasize** teamwork as a means to a solution as opposed to winning

Each game provides everything you need to conduct the activity including instructions, materials, time requirements, and reproducible worksheets or material templates. Each is categorized into one of these topics: change, communication, conflict resolution, data analysis, decision making, leadership, perception, problem solving, strategic planning, and time pressure.

Use these games to enhance cooperation, resourcefulness, decision making, efficiency, and initiative in your team today!

Working Together / **Code 0354X** / 224 pages / paperbound / **$39.95**

Start your training on the right track and keep it there!

Getting Together
Icebreakers and Group Energizers

Lorraine L. Ukens

These brief, interactive games and activities raise your participants' awareness and prepare them to learn something new. Designed to be fun and energizing, the activities help people overcome the initial anxiety common among new acquaintances or in group situations.

Use these games to:

- **Promote** interaction
- **Introduce** your topic
- **Ease** anxieties regarding sensitive or emotional issues
- **Form** partnerships or teams during the session
- **Help** people feel comfortable with the environment, the topic to be discussed, and one another
- **Gain** control of a group
- **Get** meetings started on a stimulating note

This collection is conveniently divided into two categories: 1) icebreakers, which encourage "mixing"; and 2) group challenges, which energize and build team cohesion.

Each game is presented in a concise and easy-to-follow format. You'll get details on objectives, material requirements, preparation, activity instructions, variations, discussion questions, group size, time requirements, and reproducible worksheets or material templates.

Use these icebreakers today to energize your group for the work ahead!

Getting Together / **Code 03558** / 224 pages / paperbound / **$39.95**

Team Games Duo / **Code 09602** / set of Working Together and Getting Together / **$69.95**

SAVE $9.95 On the set

TO ORDER, CALL FREE: 800-274-4434

OR FAX FREE: 800-569-0443

More Great Resources from Jossey-Bass/Pfeiffer!

Earthquake Survival
Activity and Leader's Guide

Here's a fun "situation" to help your teams quickly improve their groups' functioning. Immediately your participants will learn functional skills that will improve their performance in the workplace.

Enjoy variety and flexibility with these three complete activities:

• "Earthquake Survival Situations" Quiz • "Things to Have" to Prepare for an Earthquake • "Things to Do" During and Immediately After an Earthquake.

The *Leader's Guide* includes instructions for administering the activities and conducting discussions, possible variations, lecturettes, and samples of all forms and handouts.

Earthquake Survival Activities / **Code 04519** / 24 pages / paperbound / **$9.95**

Leader's Guide / **Code 04500** / 48 pages / paperbound / **$17.95**

Lost at Sea
Simulation and Leader's Manual

In this classic simulation, participants work individually, then as a group, to assess 15 items salvaged from a yachting accident, based on their value for survival. Results are compared with the expert rankings supplied by the U.S. Merchant Marines. Through self-scoring, the group immediately sees how well they performed.

The *Leader's Manual* offers instructions for facilitating the activity.

In this simulation, a group is stranded on a rubber life raft with minimal supplies including: • Fishing kit • Mosquito netting • Shark repellant • Shaving mirror • Two chocolate bars • And 10 other items.

Lost at Sea Simulation / **Code 89S** / 7 pages / **$6.95**

Leader's Manual / **Code 543** / 10 pages / **$17.95**

Wilderness Survival
Simulation and Leader's Manual

This survival activity poses 12 situations that someone lost in a wilderness might encounter—snakes, bears, an early snow, and other potentially life-threatening scenarios. Participants make individual then group decisions about how to survive each situation. These decisions are compared with those of expert naturalists.

The *Leader's Manual* offers instructions for facilitating the activity.

There are many life-threatening encounters in this mythical wilderness. How well will your group work together to survive?

Wilderness Survival Simulation / **Code 89R** / 10 pages / **$6.95**

Leader's Manual / **Code 541** / 10 pages / **$17.95**

 TO ORDER, CALL FREE: 800-274-4434   **OR FAX FREE: 800-569-0443**

More Great Resources from Jossey-Bass/Pfeiffer!

"A must-read for anyone who wants training to be effective and engaging."

—Sivasailam Thiagarajan, author, Games by Thiagi

Active Training

A Handbook of Techniques, Designs, Case Examples, and Tips

Mel Silberman

One of the most comprehensive texts on training ever compiled, *Active Training* shows you how to teach adults the way they learn best: by doing. It will help you effectively design and conduct experientially based training programs in public- and private-sector organizations—whether you are a novice trainer or seasoned professional.

This handbook is packed with information to help you create new training programs, modify existing courses, and combine a variety of facilitation techniques to conduct any training program more successfully. It includes over 200 designs and case examples drawn from more than 45 training professionals.

It leads you through:

- Assessing the training group
- Developing training objectives
- Using experiential learning approaches
- Conducting presentations and discussions
- Planning, designing, and sequencing training activities
- Providing for "back-on-the job" application
- Gaining leadership of a training group
- Concluding and evaluating training programs

Active Training is a complete guide to experiential learning techniques, illustrated by hundreds of examples. Use it to enhance all your training interventions.

Active Training / **Code 09084** / 284 pages / hardbound / **$44.95**

"Silberman's book proves that learning can be fun. Its usable, practical ideas make training come alive!"

—Edward E. Scannell, coauthor, Games Trainers Play series

101 Ways to Make Training Active

Mel Silberman

These proven, generic activities will enliven your sessions and deepen learning and retention—no matter what you're teaching.

This active training field guide provides activities useful for:

- Involving participants
- Promoting back-on-the-job application
- Facilitating team learning
- Reviewing program content
- Developing skills . . . and more!

You'll also get 160 training tips about: • meeting participant expectations • regaining control of the group • making lectures active • forming groups ... and more!

Easily slip any of these 101 strategies into any training you are conducting and watch your training come alive!

Contents

The Nuts and Bolts of Active Training: 160 Tips • How to Get Active Participation from the Start • Team-Building Strategies • On-the-Spot Assessment Strategies • Immediate Learning Involvement Strategies • How to Teach Information, Skills, and Attitudes Actively • Full-Class Learning • Stimulating Discussion • Prompting Questions • Team Learning • Peer Teaching • Independent Learning • Effective Learning • Skill Development • How to Make Training Unforgettable • Reviewing Strategies • Self-Assessment • Application Planning • Final Sentiments • Index to Case Examples

101 Ways to Make Training Active / **Code 04756** / 304 pages / paperbound / **$39.95**

 TO ORDER, CALL FREE: 800-274-4434   **OR FAX FREE: 800-569-0443**

More Great Resources from Jossey-Bass/Pfeiffer!

Now anyone can develop and lead a successful team with these experiential activities!

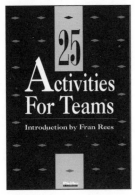

25 Activities for Teams

Fran Rees

25 Activities for Teams is a useful collection of activities and assessment tools for leading and developing high-performing work teams. Designed to complement the popular *How to Lead Work Teams,* this resource can also stand alone to help team leaders get everyone actively involved in the team's development.

Reinforcing Fran Rees' LEAD model, the activities in this book will help the team leader:

- **Lead** with a clear purpose
- **Empower** participants
- **Aim** for consensus
- **Direct** the process

25 Activities for Teams is a valuable resource that promotes fun, experiential, team learning. Best of all, it can be used by even novice team leaders and facilitators or by professional trainers. This collection brings together exercises from a variety of resources that will help teams develop skills, build cohesiveness, and accomplish important tasks.

Team leaders will use this practical resource to energize team meetings and keep them on track for maximum results.

....

25 Activities for Teams / **Code 1033** / paperbound / 108 pages / **$34.95** / Quantity Pricing **U**

Improve group results as a successful leader-facilitator

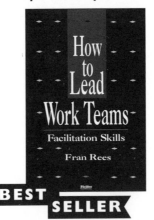

How to Lead Work Teams
Facilitation Skills

Fran Rees

Reap the benefits of a more facilitative, participative style of leadership with *How to Lead Work Teams*. You'll develop the skills to increase cooperation and job satisfaction, raise productivity and quality levels, and gain a more favorable view of your leadership abilities through facilitation.

It shows you how to:

- **Involve** others, build consensus, and get commitment
- **Help** others solve problems and make decisions
- **Use** the knowledge and experience of all employees

Get your copy today!

....

How to Lead Work Teams / **Code 659** / paperbound / 161 pages / **$24.95** / Quantity Pricing **O**

SAVE $9.90 On the set

....

Rees Team Trio / **Code 11518** / Set of How to Lead Work Teams, 25 Activities for Teams, Teamwork from Start to Finish / 3 paperbound books / **$74.95**

Show your team how to chart its own course, evaluate its progress, and self-correct.

Teamwork from Start to Finish
10 Steps to Results!

Fran Rees

Many books talk about teamwork, but few address the actual process of creating and managing effective teams. You'll learn to approach teamwork as a journey with a beginning, middle, and satisfying end. Find out how to construct a blueprint to carry your team along.

Discover the two factors essential for well-functioning teams:

- **Getting** work done
- **Building** and maintaining the spirit and momentum of the team

Frequently teams are built and challenged to work as a unit, but the team members aren't clear about what steps to take and when to take them. Keep your team from becoming confused, frustrated, and ultimately giving up. Develop step-by-step procedures to get work done!

Create teams that work together to increase productivity, improve quality, and achieve high levels of customer satisfaction.

....

Teamwork from Start to Finish / **Code 10619** / paperbound / 224 pages / **$24.95** / Quantity Pricing **O**

 TO ORDER, CALL FREE: 800-274-4434   **OR FAX FREE: 800-569-0443**